W9-ALT-036

Language
Arts

Grade 1

Flash Kids™

Harcourt
Family Learning™

© 2005 by Flash Kids
Adapted from *Language Arts, Grade 1*
© 2003 by Harcourt Achieve
Licensed under special arrangement with Harcourt Achieve.

Illustrated by Hector Borlasca

Harcourt Family Learning and Design is a trademark of Harcourt, Inc.
All rights reserved. No part of this book may be used or reproduced in any
manner whatsoever without the written permission of the Publisher.

ISBN: 978-1-4114-0409-0

Please submit all inquiries to FlashKids@bn.com

Printed and bound in China

Flash Kids
A Division of Barnes & Noble
122 Fifth Avenue
New York, NY 10011

Dear Parent,

This book was developed to help your child improve the language skills he or she needs to succeed. The book emphasizes skills in the key areas of:

- grammar
- punctuation
- vocabulary
- writing
- research

The lessons included in the book provide many opportunities for your child to practice and apply important language and writing skills. These skills will help your child improve his or her communication abilities, excel in all academic areas, and increase his or her scores on standardized tests.

About the Book

The book is divided into six units:

- Parts of Speech
- Sentences
- Mechanics
- Vocabulary and Usage
- Writing
- Research Skills

Your child can work through each unit of the book, or you can pinpoint areas for extra practice. Many pages contain information boxes about the concept presented on the page. The best approach would be to read this information to the child, then let the child complete the exercises on the page.

Lessons have specific instructions and examples and are designed for your child to complete independently. Grammar lessons range from using nouns and verbs to writing better sentences. Writing exercises range from the personal story to the book report. With this practice, your child will gain extra confidence as he or she works on daily school lessons or standardized tests.

A thorough answer key is also provided so you may check the quality of answers.

A Step toward Success

Practice may not always make perfect, but it is certainly a step in the right direction. The activities in this book are an excellent way to ensure greater success for your child.

Table of Contents

Unit 3: Mechanics

Unit 4: Vocabulary and Usage

Unit 5: Writing

Unit 6: Research Skills

Naming Words

Naming words are called **nouns.**
Nouns name people, places, and things.
Examples:

man   house   boat

DIRECTIONS Look at each picture. Say the naming word under each picture. Then, write the naming word on the line.

1.  boy

boy

2. girl

girl

3.  dog

dog

4.  cat

cat

More Naming Words

Remember, naming words are called nouns. Nouns name people, places, and things.

DIRECTIONS Read the word in each box. Look at each picture. Then, write the naming word for each picture on the line.

1.

man

Man

2.

baby

baby

3.

school

school

4.

store

store

5.

car

Car

6.

fish

fish

Naming Words for People

Some nouns name people.
Examples:

    sister   teacher   dad

DIRECTIONS Read the words in the box. Look at each picture. Name each person. Write a word from the box.

farmer   doctor   cook   worker

1. doctor

2. farmer

3. worker

4. cook

Naming Words for Animals

Some nouns name animals.
Examples:
   pig
   horse
   whale

DIRECTIONS Complete each sentence. Write a word from the box.

frog	fish	dog	cat	bird	fox

1. A _The fish_ swims in the sea.

2. A _The frog_ jumps out of a pond.

3. A _The fox_ runs in the woods.

4. A _The bird_ flies in the sky.

5. A _The dog_ barks at strangers.

6. A _The cat_ meows.

Naming Words for Places

Some nouns name places.
Examples:

     city   beach   library

DIRECTIONS   Read the words in the box. Look at each picture. Name the place. Write a word from the box.

house	farm	lake	park

1. lake

2. house

3. park

4. farm

Naming Words for Things

Some nouns name things.
Examples:

    toy

    chair

    shoes

DIRECTIONS   **Complete each sentence. Write a word from the box.**

cup	hat	bed	apple	crayons	box

1. I drink juice from a _____cup_____.

2. I use _____crayons_____ for coloring.

3. I eat an _____apple_____ with lunch.

4. I sleep in a _____bed_____.

5. I wear a _____hat_____ on my head.

6. I keep my toys in a _____box_____.

Practice with Naming Words

A noun can name a person, place, thing, or animal.
Examples:

   mother   grass   duck   pencil

DIRECTIONS Read the clues. Fill in the puzzle with words from the box.

   car   snake   teacher   tree   house

Down

1. This kind of plant has a trunk.

2. A family can live in this place.

4. You can drive in this thing.

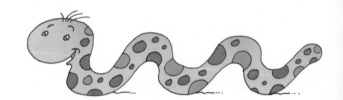

Across

1. This person works in a school.

3. This animal is long and thin.

				4. C		
1. T	e	a	c	h	e	r
r				2. o		
e				u		
e				3. s	n	a	k	e
				e		

Two Kinds of Naming Words

Some words name common things.
These words are called **common nouns**.
Examples:

    child   park   story

Some words name special things. These
words are called **proper nouns**. They begin
with capital letters.
Examples:

    Sam   Peace Park   "The Red Pony"

DIRECTIONS Read each sentence. Circle the special name in each
sentence. Then, write the special name on the line.

1. That boy is Chris. _____ boy Chris

2. That girl is Lina. _____ Lina

3. My friend is Lee Chin. _____ Lee Chin

4. I live on Main Street. _____ I Main Street

5. I read "All About Worms." _____ All About Worms

Special Names of People and Places

The special name of a person begins with a capital letter.
The special title of a person begins with a capital letter.
The special name of a place begins with a capital letter.

Examples:

Katie

Dr. Jones

New York City

DIRECTIONS Write each special name or title correctly. Be sure to use capital letters.

1. This book is for sam. _____ Sam

2. mr. Sosa has a new car. _____ Mr. Sosa

3. My friend goes to parker school. _____ Parker

4. We live on bakers road. _____ We Bakers

Practice with Proper Names

A special name of a person begins with a capital letter. The special title of a person begins with a capital letter. The special name of a place begins with a capital letter.

Examples:

Ms. Reed

Chicago

Lucy

DIRECTIONS Answer each question using the special name of a person or a place. Remember to use capital letters.

1. What is your name? _____ ~~Name~~ An Sim

2. What is your teacher's name? _____ ~~Teacher~~ Mrs. Willydson

3. What is the name of your school? _____ ~~school~~ Crabapul mcloud's

4. What is the name of your town or city? _____ ~~City~~ Landi richmin hil

5. What is your best friend's name? _____ ~~friend~~ mommy

DIRECTIONS On another piece of paper, draw a picture of one person or place you wrote about above.

Naming One and More Than One

A naming word can name **one**.
A naming word can name **more than one**.
Many naming words add <u>s</u> to name more than one.
Example:

    one **cat**

    two **cat<u>s</u>**

DIRECTIONS   Write the naming word in ( ) to complete each sentence.

1. I see two _birds_.
        (bird, birds)

2. I see one _bug_.
        (bug, bugs)

3. I see two _girls_.
        (girl, girls)

4. I see one _dog_.
        (dog, dogs)

5. I see three _frogs_.
        (frog, frogs)

Practice with Naming More Than One

Many naming words add <u>s</u> to name more than one.
Example:
    one **bird**
    two **bird<u>s</u>**

DIRECTIONS **Read the first sentence. Finish the second sentence to show more than one.**

1. We planted a new tree.

   Now we have six _____trees_____ in our yard.

2. Ruby picked one flower.

   Ned picked two _____flowers_____ .

3. Dad had one seed.

   Mom had two _____seeds_____ .

4. We found one nest.

   They found three _____nests_____ .

I and Me

The words <u>I</u> and <u>me</u> take the place of some naming words. Use <u>I</u> in the naming part of a sentence. The word <u>I</u> is always written as a capital letter. Use <u>me</u> in the telling part of a sentence.

Examples:

I have a new dog.

The dog licks **me**.

DIRECTIONS Write <u>I</u> or <u>me</u> to complete each sentence.

1. _____I_____ am a big red rooster.

2. Can you find ____me____?

3. _____I_____ am not in the henhouse.

4. Surprise! ____I̶ ̶m̶____ am in the garden!

5. Now you can see ____me____.

Practice with I and Me

Remember, use <u>I</u> in the naming part of a sentence. The word <u>I</u> is always written as a capital letter. Use <u>me</u> in the telling part of a sentence.

Examples:

I like pizza.

Will you make a pizza for **me**?

DIRECTIONS   Write <u>I</u> or <u>me</u> to complete each sentence.

1. _____I_____ like to skate.

2. Mom takes _____me_____ to the pond on Saturdays.

3. _____I_____ practice all day.

4. Mom claps for _____me_____ .

5. _____I_____ have a lot of fun.

We and They

The words <u>we</u> and <u>they</u> take the place of some naming words.
Use <u>we</u> and <u>they</u> in the naming part of a sentence.
Examples:
> <u>Jim and I</u> will talk.
> **We** will talk.
>
> <u>Kay and Chris</u> will talk.
> **They** will talk.

DIRECTIONS ➤ Rewrite each sentence. Write <u>We</u> or <u>They</u> to take the place of the underlined names.

1. <u>Sam and I</u> are here.

We are here

2. <u>Kay and Amy</u> are not here.

We are

3. <u>Kim and I</u> will play ball.

4. <u>Ann, Pat, and Chad</u> found a kitten.

Practice with <u>We</u> and <u>They</u>

Remember, use <u>we</u> and <u>they</u> in the naming part of a sentence.
Examples:

<u>John and I</u> are best friends.
We are best friends.

<u>Olivia and Adam</u> are twins.
They are twins.

○ ○○ ○ ○○ ○ ○○○ ○ ○○ ○ ○○ ○ ○○○ ○ ○○ ○ ○○ ○ ○○ ○ ○○○ ○ ○○ ○ ○○ ○ ○○ ○ ○

DIRECTIONS ➤ Rewrite each sentence. Write <u>We</u> or <u>They</u> to take the place of the underlined names.

1. <u>Evan and Alan</u> are brothers.

   They are brothers

2. <u>Emma and I</u> are sisters.

   We are sisters

3. <u>Evan and Emma</u> are in second grade.

   They are in second grade.

4. <u>Alan and I</u> are in first grade.

   We are in first grade

He, She, and It

The words he, she, and it take the place of some naming words.
Use he for a man or a boy.
Use she for a woman or a girl.
Use it for an animal or a thing.
Examples:

He rows the boat.

She rides in **it**.

DIRECTIONS Rewrite each sentence. Use **He**, **She**, or **It** in place of the underlined words.

1. Amy likes to write.

She likes to write.

2. John likes to read.

Johe likes to read.

3. The book is on the table.

It is on the table.

4. Jenna saw the bird.

She saw the brid

Practice with <u>He</u>, <u>She</u>, and <u>It</u>

Remember, use <u>he</u> for a man or a boy.
Use <u>she</u> for a woman or a girl.
Use <u>it</u> for an animal or a thing.
Examples:
   My dad is nice. **He** is also funny.
   My sister is little. **She** is only three years old.
   Our house is big. **It** is blue.

DIRECTIONS — **Read the first sentence. Then complete the second sentence using <u>He</u>, <u>She</u>, or <u>It</u>.**

1. My dad works at a school. ___he___ is a teacher.

2. The school is big. ___it___ has many classrooms.

3. My mom works in a hospital. ___She___ is a doctor.

4. The hospital is on Main Street. ___he___ has ten floors.

5. Mom lets me visit her at work. ___She___ shows me her office.

6. Dad takes me to his school. ___he___ shows me his classroom.

Action Words

An **action word** tells what someone or something does. Action words are called **verbs**.

Examples:

Tom **sleeps**.
Birds **fly**.
Dogs **bark**.

DIRECTIONS ⟩ **Complete each sentence. Write an action word from the box.**

talks	ride	eats	sing	waves

1. The girl _____ eats _____ the food.

2. Dad _____ waves _____ good-bye.

3. The boy _____ talks _____ on the phone.

4. We _____ sing _____ songs.

5. We _____ ride _____ our bikes.

Action Words

Using Clear Action Words

Some action words tell exactly how people and things move.
Examples:

The dog **races** across the grass.
The horse **gallops** across the field.

 Complete each sentence. Choose the word in ( ) that tells exactly how each animal moves. Write the new sentence.

1. The fish (swims, stays) in the lake.

The fish swims in the lake

2. The rabbit (goes, hops) up and down.

The rabbit hops up and down

3. The snake (sits, crawls) on the ground.

The snake crawls on the ground

4. The birds (fly, move) in the sky.

The birds fly in the sky

Action Word Web

There are many action words. Sometimes,
more than one word can tell about an action.
Examples:

> Cari **goes** to school.
> Cari **walks** to school.
> Cari **runs** to school.
> Cari **skips** to school.

DIRECTIONS Complete the word web. Write action words to replace the word <u>talk</u> in the sentence.

replied

said

The children <u>talk</u> about the wind.

whind

sqeted

DIRECTIONS Write a sentence. Use an action word from the web.

Action Words with One or More Than One

Action words can tell what one person or thing does. Action words can also tell what more than one person or thing does.

Add <u>s</u> to an action word that tells about one person or thing.

Example:

The two boys **play** ball.

The one boy **plays** ball.

DIRECTIONS **Complete each sentence. Write an action word.**

1. The two girls The two girls climeds rope.

   The one girl The one girl climed rope.

2. The balls _____ slowly.

   The ball _____ slowly.

3. The dogs _____ .

   The dog _____ .

Action Words About Now

An action word can tell about now. Action words that tell about one person, place, or thing end with <u>s</u>. Action words that tell about more than one person, place, or thing do not end with <u>s</u>.
Examples:

Ray **helps** his dad.

Sam and Sara **throw** the ball.

> **DIRECTIONS** Circle the action word in each sentence.

1. The sun shines all day long.

2. The seeds grow in the garden.

3. The frog hops over the log.

> **DIRECTIONS** Complete each sentence. Choose the correct action word in ( ). Write the word on the line.

4. The flowers _____ water.
   (need, needs)

5. The boy _____ some water.
   (get, gets)

More Action Words About Now

Remember, action words that tell about one person, place, or thing end with <u>s</u>. Action words that tell about more than one person, place, or thing do not end with <u>s</u>.

Examples:

David **drink<u>s</u>** a glass of milk.

David and his sister **wash** the dishes.

DIRECTIONS ▸ Finish the story using words from the box.

welcomes	smile	puts	walk	thinks	eats	finds

Today is the first day of school. Madison _____

pancakes. She _____ on her dress and shoes.

She and her sister _____ to school.

Madison _____ her classroom.

The teacher _____ the students.

The children _____ at their new teacher.

Madison _____ it will be a good year.

Action Words About the Past

An action word can tell about the past. Some action words that tell about the past end with <u>ed</u>.
Examples:

A mother duck **walk<u>ed</u>** across the grass.
She **quack<u>ed</u>** for the little ducks.

DIRECTIONS Complete each sentence. Choose the word in ( ) that tells about the past. Write the new sentence.

1. Two little ducks (plays, played) in the water.

_____

_____

2. The mother duck (look, looked) at them.

_____

_____

3. Two little ducks (jumped, jump) out of the water.

_____

_____

4. They all (walk, walked) away.

_____

_____

Practice with Action Words

Remember, action words can tell about now.
Example:

    I **play** checkers with my brother.

Action words can also tell about the past.
Example:

    Last night I **played** checkers with my sister.

DIRECTIONS ➤ **Read each sentence. Choose the correct word in ( ) to complete the sentence.**

1. Last summer we _____ in the lake.
                      (fish, fished)

2. Last night Sara _____ TV.
                    (watch, watched)

3. Now Harry and Sam _____ to music.
                    (listen, listened)

4. Last year Anna _____ a picture.
                    (paint, painted)

5. Mike bought food to _____ for dinner.
                    (cook, cooked)

Using Is and Are

Use <u>is</u> to tell about what one person or thing is doing now. Use <u>are</u> to tell about what more than one one person or thing are doing now.
Examples:

Jack **is** sick today.

Jack's friends **are** sick, too.

DIRECTIONS ➤ Complete each sentence. Write <u>is</u> or <u>are</u>.

1. He _____ my father.

2. She _____ my mother.

3. They _____ in the garden.

4. Sue and I _____ in the garden, too.

5. The flowers _____ pretty.

6. Our dog _____ black and white.

Practice with Is and Are

Remember, use <u>is</u> to tell about what one person or thing is doing now. Use <u>are</u> to tell about what two or more people or things are doing now.

Examples:

He **is** running very fast.

The other children **are** running, too.

DIRECTIONS ▷ **Write <u>is</u> or <u>are</u> in each blank to complete the story.**

Luke _____ very smart. We _____

best friends. We _____ in first grade. Mr. Jackson

_____ our teacher. We _____

learning about birds. Luke _____ making a birdhouse.

Using Was and Were

Use <u>was</u> to tell about one person or thing in the past.
Use <u>were</u> to tell about more than one person or thing in the past.
Examples:
    One cat **was** on the mat.
    Two cats **were** on the bench.

DIRECTIONS ➤ Complete each sentence. Write <u>was</u> or <u>were</u>.

1. I _____ at the lake.

2. Carl and Bert _____ there, too.

3. We _____ going to sleep.

4. The rain _____ a big surprise.

5. The tent _____ all wet.

6. Dad _____ calling us.

Practice with <u>Was</u> and <u>Were</u>

Remember, use <u>was</u> to tell about what one person or thing did in the past. Use <u>were</u> to tell about what two or more people or things did in the past.

Examples:

Ava **was** in her bedroom.

Tom and Ben **were** in the yard.

DIRECTIONS ➤ **Write <u>was</u> or <u>were</u> in each blank to complete the story.**

Tyler and Haley _____ moving to a new

house. Mom and Dad _____ filling the truck.

Haley _____ putting her toys in a box.

Tyler _____ cleaning his room. The children

_____ ready to see their

new home. They _____

also sad to leave their old house.

Using See, Come, and Run

Use see, come, and run to tell about something that happens now.
Use saw, came, and ran to tell about something
that happened in the past.
Examples:

    I **see** a red balloon now.

    Dad **came** home yesterday.

 **DIRECTIONS** Complete each sentence. Circle the correct action word in ( ).

1. Last night Kim (run, ran) to the store.

2. Now I (run, ran) to the store.

3. Last week Bob (see, saw) a new movie.

4. Yesterday Tina (come, came) to my house.

5. Now Tina and Kim (come, came) to my house.

DIRECTIONS Write sentences. Use the word in ( ) in your sentence.

6. (see)

_____

- -

_____

7. (run)

_____

- -

_____

Practice with See, Come, and Run

Remember, use <u>see</u>, <u>come</u>, and <u>run</u> to tell about something that happens now. Use <u>saw</u>, <u>came</u>, and <u>ran</u> to tell about something that happened in the past.

Examples:

Yesterday I **ran** home.

Today I **run** to school.

DIRECTIONS ▷ **Complete each sentence with a word from the box.**

see	saw	come	came	run	ran

1. My grandparents _____ to visit last week.

2. Can you _____ the rainbow now?

3. Now Lisa and I _____ to the store.

4. Wes _____ in the race yesterday.

5. Last night I _____ a good show.

6. Can Eric _____ to my house right now?

Using Go and Went

The words go and <u>went</u> are action words. Use go to tell about now.
Use <u>went</u> to tell about the past.
Examples:
    Today we **go** to school.
    Last week we **went** to the beach.

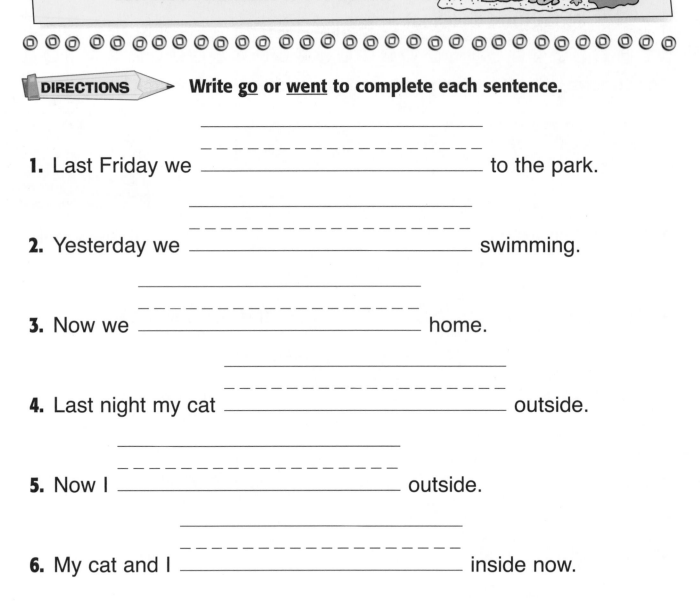

DIRECTIONS   **Write go or <u>went</u> to complete each sentence.**

1. Last Friday we _____ to the park.

2. Yesterday we _____ swimming.

3. Now we _____ home.

4. Last night my cat _____ outside.

5. Now I _____ outside.

6. My cat and I _____ inside now.

Practice with Go and Went

Remember, use <u>go</u> to tell about something happening now.
Use <u>went</u> to tell about something that happened
in the past.
Examples:

Last year we **went** to visit my aunt.
Now we **go** to visit my grandmother.

DIRECTIONS Write go or <u>went</u> to complete each sentence.

1. Last year we _____ to New York on a plane.

2. Now we _____ to Texas in a car.

3. Last year I _____ to Turner School.

4. Now I _____ to Park Lane School.

5. Now Kara and Ted _____ to the pool to swim.

6. Last week they _____ to the track to run.

Contractions with Not

A **contraction** is a word made by joining two words. An **apostrophe** (') shows where a letter or letters are left out. Many contractions are made with the word <u>not</u>.

Examples:

do + not = **don't**

had + not = **hadn't**

will + not = **won't**

DIRECTIONS ▷ **Complete each sentence. Write the words in ( ) as a contraction. Use an apostrophe (') in your contraction.**

1. I _____ like snakes.
   (do not)

2. I _____ go near a snake.
   (will not)

3. You _____ make me touch one.
   (can not)

4. Zack _____ here.
   (is not)

5. I _____ seen him all day.
   (have not)

6. You _____ go there.
   (should not)

Practice with Contractions

Remember, a contraction is a word made by joining two words.
An apostrophe shows where a letter or letters are left out.
Examples:

do + not = **don't**

can + not = **can't**

is + not = **isn't**

 **DIRECTIONS** ▷ **Complete each sentence with a word from the box.**

haven't	shouldn't	can't	isn't	don't	won't

1. You _____ swim alone.

2. I _____ been to China.

3. It _____ time to go yet.

4. She _____ tie her shoes.

5. He _____ tell anyone the secret.

6. Please _____ throw that!

Words That Tell Where

Some words tell where.
Example:
    The frog is **on** the log.

DIRECTIONS Complete each sentence. Use a word from the box.

in	under	out	on	up

1. The cat is looking _____ the box.

2. The cat sat _____ the chair.

3. The cat is _____ the chair.

4. The balloon goes _____.

5. A gopher peeks _____ of its hole.

Practice with Words That Tell Where

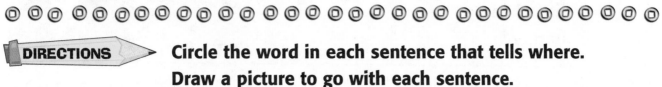

Some words tell where.
Example:
> The bird is **in** the tree.

DIRECTIONS ▶ Circle the word in each sentence that tells where.
Draw a picture to go with each sentence.

1. A bug is on the rug.	**2.** The kite goes up.
3. The boy is under the umbrella.	**4.** The flower is in a pot.

Describing Words

Describing words tell about naming words.

Examples:

> **three** birds
> **tall** boy
> **little** bear
> **happy** girl

DIRECTIONS ▸ Circle each describing word. Then, write it on the line.

1. green frog

_____

2. loud noise

_____

3. wet dog

_____

4. two girls

_____

5. blue water

_____

6. funny clown

_____

Describing Words About Feelings

Some describing words tell how people **feel**.
Examples:
    Yesterday Sandi was **sad**.
    Now Sandi is **happy**.

DIRECTIONS Complete each sentence. Choose a word from the box. Write it on the line.

hungry	sleepy	glad	sick	angry

1. When Freddy is _____, he takes a nap.

2. When Freddy is _____, he goes to the doctor.

3. When Freddy is _____, he eats.

4. When Freddy sees his friend, he is _____.

5. When Freddy is _____, he is not happy.

Describing Words About Size and Shape

Some describing words tell about **size** and **shape**.
Examples:

big dog
square book

DIRECTIONS ▶ Answer each question. Choose a word in ( ). Write the word on the line.

1. What size is a whale? _____
(sad, big)

2. What size is an ant? _____
(small, sleepy)

3. What size is a tree? _____
(green, tall)

4. What shape is a ball? _____
(round, blue)

DIRECTIONS ▶ Write a sentence. Use a describing word about size or shape.

5. _____

Describing Words About Color

Some describing words tell about **color**.
Examples:
    blue water
    black cat
    gray whale

DIRECTIONS Complete each sentence. Choose a describing word from the box. Write the word on the line.

blue	yellow	pink	white	green	red

1. The grass is _____.

2. The flowers are _____.

3. That bird is bright _____.

4. Watch it fly into the _____ sky.

5. It is flying into a _____ cloud.

6. I am flying a _____ kite.

Describing Words About Numbers

Some describing words tell **how many**.
Examples:

   one nose
   five toes

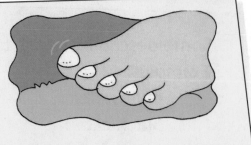

DIRECTIONS Complete each sentence. Use a number word from the box. Use the picture to help you.

one	two	three	four	five
six	seven	eight	nine	ten

1. I have _____ carton of milk.

2. I have _____ cookies.

3. I see _____ balloons.

4. The cake has _____ candles.

5. I see _____ pumpkins.

Describing Words About Numbers

Describing Words About Taste and Smell

Some describing words tell how things **taste**.
Some describing words tell how things **smell**.
Examples:
This is **salty** popcorn.
The flower smells **sweet**.

DIRECTIONS Circle each describing word. Then, write it on the line.

1. The lemons taste sour. _____

2. The bread smells fresh. _____

3. I like salty peanuts. _____

4. I smell a smoky fire. _____

DIRECTIONS Write a sentence. Use a describing word about taste or smell.

5. _____

Describing Words About Feel and Sound

Some describing words tell how things **feel**.
Some describing words tell how things **sound**.
Examples:

Ice cream feels **cold**.
The school bell is **loud**.

DIRECTIONS ▷ Complete each sentence. Choose a word in ( ) that tells about feel or sound. Write the word on the line.

1. The kitten is _____.
(soft, small)

2. I like to read in _____ rooms.
(two, quiet)

3. The sunshine is _____.
(long, hot)

4. I put _____ ice in my drink.
(cold, tall)

5. The ticking clock is _____.
(wet, noisy)

Describing Words About the Weather

Some describing words tell about the **weather**.

Example:

We had **stormy** weather yesterday.

DIRECTIONS Look at each picture. Complete each sentence. Choose a weather word from the box. Write it on the line.

| rainy | snowy | sunny | windy | cloudy |

1. It is a _____ day.

2. It is a _____ day.

3. It is a _____ day.

4. It is a _____ day.

5. It is a _____ day.

Using Describing Words

Remember, describing words tell about naming words.

DIRECTIONS Write a describing word for each naming word.

1.
toad

_____

_____

2.
cow

_____

_____

3.
chick

_____

_____

4.
whale

_____

_____

5.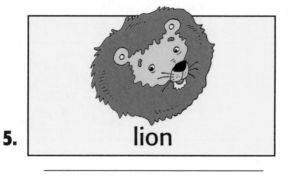
lion

_____

_____

6.
rabbit

_____

_____

Describing Words

Practice with Describing Words

Remember, describing words tell about naming words.

DIRECTIONS Write a sentence for each describing word.

1. red

2. fast

3. funny

4. rainy

5. small

DIRECTIONS Draw a picture to go with one of the sentences you wrote.

Describing Words That Compare

Some describing words tell how two things are different. Add <u>er</u> to a describing word to tell how two things are different.

Some describing words tell how more than two things are different. Add <u>est</u> to a describing word to tell how more than two things are different.

Examples:

small, smaller, smallest

The cat is **small**.

The mouse is **smaller** than the cat.

The ant is the **smallest** of all.

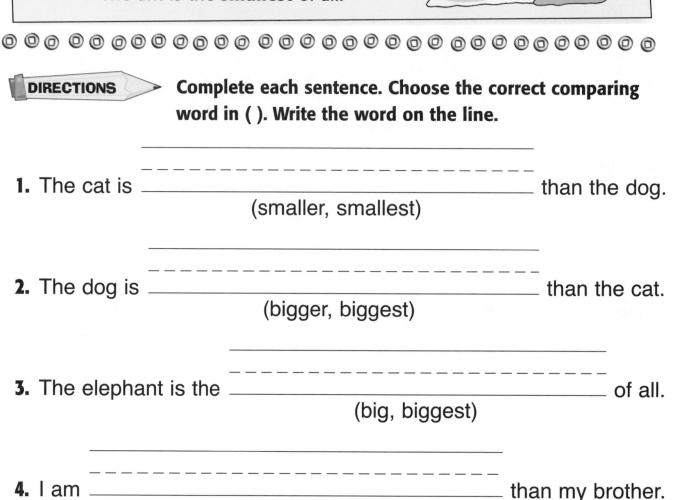

DIRECTIONS Complete each sentence. Choose the correct comparing word in ( ). Write the word on the line.

1. The cat is _____ than the dog.
(smaller, smallest)

2. The dog is _____ than the cat.
(bigger, biggest)

3. The elephant is the _____ of all.
(big, biggest)

4. I am _____ than my brother.
(tall, taller)

More Describing Words That Compare

DIRECTIONS Answer each question. Circle the correct picture.

1. Which goat is <u>bigger</u>?

2. Which bridge is <u>longer</u>?

3. Which is the <u>tallest</u> tree of all?

4. Which is the <u>highest</u> building of all?

Using A and An

Use <u>a</u> before words that begin with a consonant sound.
Use <u>an</u> before words that begin with a vowel sound.
The vowels are <u>a</u>, <u>e</u>, <u>i</u>, <u>o</u>, and <u>u</u>.
Examples:

    a car, **a** skate

    an ant, **an** egg

DIRECTIONS Read each word. Write <u>a</u> or <u>an</u> on the line.

1. _____ tent

2. _____ train

3. _____ orange

4. _____ owl

5. _____ book

6. _____ bike

7. _____ apple

8. _____ oak tree

Practice with A and An

Remember, use <u>a</u> before words that begin with a consonant sound. Use <u>an</u> before words that begin with a vowel sound. The vowels are <u>a</u>, <u>e</u>, <u>i</u>, <u>o</u>, and <u>u</u>.
Example:

   an apple, **a** cat

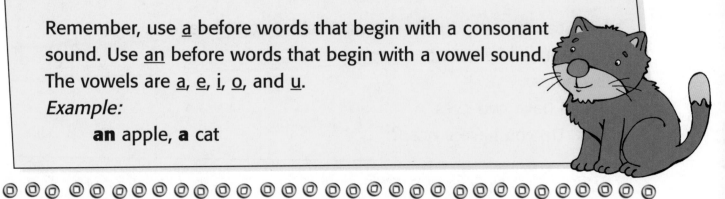

 **DIRECTIONS** Look at each word in the word box. If it begins with a vowel, write it in the <u>an</u> side of the chart. If it begins with a consonant, write it in the <u>a</u> side of the chart.

uncle	radio	bear	airplane	fish
ape	lamp	inch	ocean	queen

a	**an**

Sentences

A **sentence** is a group of words. It tells a complete idea.
A sentence begins with a capital letter.
Examples:

I have two eyes.

Do you have a nose?

DIRECTIONS Underline the groups of words that are sentences.

1. I see a lion.
see a lion.

2. throws the ball.
Jan throws the ball.

3. I hear a bird.
a bird.

DIRECTIONS Write the sentences correctly.

4. my cat can jump.

_____

- -

_____

5. the dog barks.

_____

- -

_____

Is It a Sentence?

Remember, a sentence tells a complete idea.
A sentence begins with a capital letter.

DIRECTIONS **Read each group of words. Write <u>yes</u> if the words are a sentence. Write <u>no</u> if the words are not a sentence.**

1. Today is my birthday.

2. have a party.

3. open the presents.

4. We will eat some cake.

5. All my friends are here.

6. play some games.

7. making ice cream.

8. My birthday party is fun.

Sentence Parts

A sentence has two parts. The **naming part** tells who or what the sentence is about.

The **telling part** tells what someone or something does.

A naming part and a telling part make a complete sentence.

Examples:

Naming Part	Telling Part
Sari	plants some seeds.
The girls	sing a song.

DIRECTIONS Underline the naming part in each sentence.

1. A frog jumped in the grass.

2. A cat saw the frog.

3. A dog ran after the cat.

DIRECTIONS Circle the telling part in each sentence.

4. Dogs chew bones.

5. Birds eat worms.

6. Jacy walks to school.

Practice with Sentence Parts

Remember, a naming part and a telling part make a complete sentence.

Example:

Naming Part	**Telling Part**
Andrew	plays drums.

DIRECTIONS → **Draw a line to match each naming part with a telling part.**

1. The fisherman   draws a picture.

2. The dancer   gets a fish.

3. The artist   helps the sick girl.

4. The doctor   spins on stage.

Naming Parts of Sentences

A sentence has a **naming part**. It tells who or what the sentence is about.
Examples:

    The friends play.   **The duck** is brown.

DIRECTIONS ▸ Read each sentence. Then, read the question. Write the answer to the question on the line.

1. Rick went to the zoo.

Who did something? _____

2. His mother went with him.

Who did something? _____

3. The bear ate some food.

What did something? _____

4. The monkey did some tricks.

What did something? _____

5. The tiger slept in its cage.

What did something? _____

6. The turtle swam in the water.

What did something? _____

Naming Parts of Sentences, page 2

Remember, the naming part tells who or what the sentence is about.

DIRECTIONS Complete each sentence. Write a naming part. Use the words in the box.

Who	What
My sister	The blue kite
Amy	The wind
	The red kite

1. _____ flies a blue kite.

2. _____ has a red kite.

3. _____ takes the kites up.

4. _____ is hard to see.

5. _____ is easy to see.

Telling Parts of Sentences

A sentence has a **telling part**. It tells
what someone or something does or is.
Examples:

Pat **plays in the grass**.
The grass **is green and tall**.

DIRECTIONS Read each sentence. Then, read the question. Write the
answer to the question on the line.

1. Anna found a puppy.

_____

What did Anna do? _____

2. The puppy ate some food.

_____

What did the puppy do? _____

3. The puppy played with Anna.

_____

What did the puppy do? _____

4. Anna named the puppy Skip.

_____

What did Anna do? _____

5. Anna threw the ball.

_____

What did Anna do? _____

6. Skip ran after the ball.

_____

What did Skip do? _____

Telling Parts of Sentences, page 2

Remember, the telling part tells what someone or something does or is.

◎◎◎◎◎◎◎◎◎◎◎◎◎◎◎◎◎◎◎◎◎◎◎◎◎◎◎◎

DIRECTIONS Complete each sentence. Write a telling part. Use the words in the box.

Telling Parts
will show you
are fun to grow
gives them light
plant seeds
waters the seeds

1. Flowers _____.

2. I _____.

3. You _____.

4. The rain _____.

5. The sun _____.

Writing Sentences with Naming Parts

Remember, the naming part tells who or what the sentence is about.

DIRECTIONS Complete each sentence. Write a naming part.

1. _____ has a bike.

2. _____ is green.

3. _____ is tall.

4. _____ found a pretty rock.

5. _____ reads a book.

6. _____ climbs a tree.

7. _____ barks at a cat.

8. _____ runs to the store.

Writing Sentences with Telling Parts

Remember, the telling part tells what someone or something does or is.

DIRECTIONS Complete each sentence. Write a telling part.

1. The man _____.

2. The cat _____.

3. The fish _____.

4. The balloon _____.

5. My friend _____.

6. The bird _____.

7. The boy _____.

8. The girl _____.

Word Order in Sentences

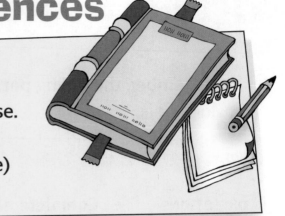

Words in a sentence are in order.
The words must be in order to make sense.
Example:

    book a Pablo gets. (makes no sense)
    Pablo gets a book. (makes sense)

DIRECTIONS ➤ **Write each sentence in correct word order.**

1. fast Jim swims

_____

- -

_____ .

2. can not swim Jane

_____

- -

_____ .

3. Mike art likes

_____

- -

_____ .

4. to town Eva walks

_____

- -

_____ .

5. Kim bird sees a

_____

- -

_____ .

6. sing The birds to me

_____

- -

_____ .

Telling Sentences

A **telling sentence** tells about something or someone. It begins
with a capital letter. It ends with a **period (.)**.
Examples:

<u>A</u> frog hops away.
<u>W</u>e try to get it.

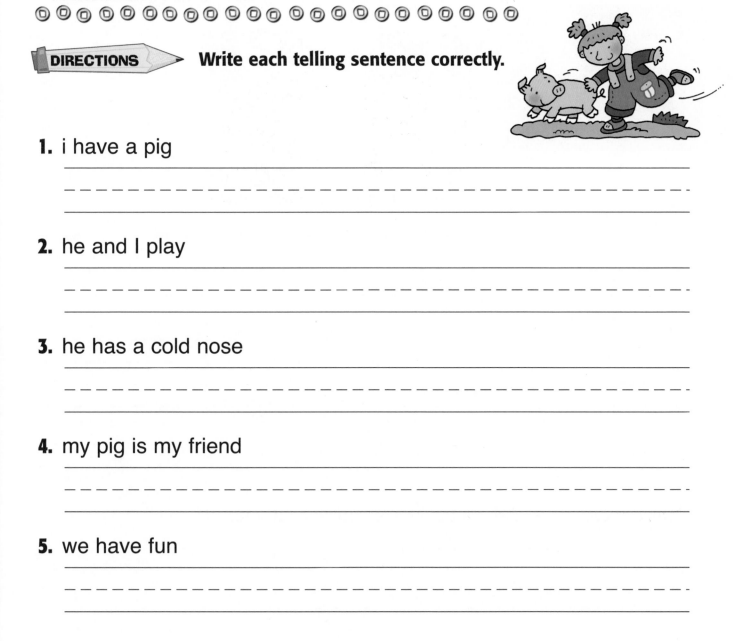

DIRECTIONS Write each telling sentence correctly.

1. i have a pig

_____

_____

2. he and I play

_____

_____

3. he has a cold nose

_____

_____

4. my pig is my friend

_____

_____

5. we have fun

_____

_____

Telling Sentences, page 2

Remember, a telling sentence tells about something or someone. It begins with a capital letter. It ends with a period (.).

DIRECTIONS ▷ **Write a sentence for each picture. Tell about the animals.**

1. _____

2. _____

DIRECTIONS ▷ **Write a telling sentence about yourself.**

3. _____

Asking Sentences

An **asking sentence** asks about something or someone. It begins with a capital letter. It ends with a **question mark (?)**.
Examples:
 How old are you?
 Do you like pets?

DIRECTIONS Write each asking sentence correctly.

1. what is your name

_____

- -

_____

2. where do you live

_____

- -

_____

3. when is your birthday

_____

- -

_____

4. do you have a pet

_____

- -

_____

5. who is your best friend

_____

- -

_____

Asking Sentences, page 2

Remember, an asking sentence asks about something or someone.
An asking sentence often begins with a question word.
Examples:

> **What** are you doing?
> **Where** have you been?

DIRECTIONS ▷ Complete each sentence. Write a question word from the box.

Question Words
Who
What
When
Where

1. _____ did the circus come to town?

2. _____ took you to the circus?

3. _____ did you see first?

4. _____ are the elephants?

5. _____ climbs the rope?

6. _____ did the clowns do?

Telling or Asking?

Remember, a telling sentence tells about something or someone.
An asking sentence asks about something or someone.
Examples:

    I have a new pencil.
    When did you get it?

DIRECTIONS   **Read each sentence. Write <u>tell</u> if it is a telling sentence. Write <u>ask</u> if it is an asking sentence.**

1. I saw a fish.

2. Where did you see it?

3. I saw it in the lake.

4. What color was the fish?

5. Who took my lunch?

6. I like to swim.

7. How cold is the water?

Writing Sentences with Describing Words

Describing words make sentences more interesting.
Example:

I saw a flower.

I saw a **pink** flower.

DIRECTIONS Complete each sentence. Add describing words.

1. Ice cream is _____.

2. I ate a _____ apple.

3. I have _____ pencils.

4. The dog is _____.

5. The cat is _____.

6. The rabbit is _____ and

_____.

Writing Sentences with

Joining Naming Parts

A sentence has a naming part. Sometimes the naming parts of two sentences can be joined. Use the word **and** to join the parts.

Example:

Turtle looked. **Fox** looked.

Turtle and Fox looked.

DIRECTIONS ➤ Join the naming parts of the sentences. Use the word **and**. Write the new sentences.

1. Turtle hid. Fox hid.

_____

_ _

_____

2. Jon played ball. Teri played ball.

_____

_ _

_____

3. Brett ate lunch. Max ate lunch.

_____

_ _

_____

4. Cat played with Duck. Frog played with Duck.

_____

_ _

_____

Joining Telling Parts

A sentence has a telling part. Sometimes the telling parts of two sentences can be joined. Use the word <u>and</u> to join the parts.
Example:

The birds **fly**. The birds **sing**.
The birds **fly** <u>and</u> **sing**.

DIRECTIONS Join the telling parts of the sentences. Use the word <u>and</u>. Write the new sentences.

1. Chet reads. Chet writes.

2. The ducks swim. The ducks quack.

3. I found a coin. I found a comb.

4. We will eat some cake. We will eat some ice cream.

Beginning Sentences with a Capital Letter

A sentence always begins with a capital letter.

Examples:

The horse ran away.   A dog ran after the horse.

I ran after the dog.

DIRECTIONS → Write each sentence correctly. Be sure to begin each sentence with a capital letter.

1. the sun is hot.

The sun is hot.

2. we will go home.

We will go home.

3. you can come with us.

You can come with us.

4. i will get some water.

I will get some water

5. do you have a cup?

Do you have a cup.

6. where is the door?

Where is the door.

The Word I

The word <u>I</u> is always written with a capital letter.
Examples:

    I have a new bike.
    Tomorrow **I** will ride to school.
    Where can **I** find a flower?

DIRECTIONS   **Answer the questions. Write sentences. Begin each sentence with <u>I can</u>.**

1. What can you ride?

_____

_____

2. What can you make?

_____

_____

3. How can you help at home?

_____

_____

4. What can you write?

_____

_____

Writing Names of People

The names of people always begin with a capital letter. The first letter in each name is a capital letter.

Examples:

Carla Cantu

Yuko Ito

Aunt Angela

Uncle Bart

DIRECTIONS   Rewrite each name. Begin each name with a capital letter.

1. pat long

2. eva ramos

3. uncle thomas

4. will smith

5. ling chung

6. mori adams

Practice with Names of People

Remember, the names of people always begin with a capital letter. The first letter in each name is a capital letter.
Example:
   Laura Lewis
Titles in a name also begin with a capital letter.
Examples:
   Mr. Li
   Dr. Green

DIRECTIONS → **Answer each question with a name. Begin each name with a capital letter.**

1. Who is your teacher? _____ Mrs. Willeamson

2. Who sits next to you at school? _____ ? _____

3. Who plays with you? _____ My fredns _____

4. Who lives with you? _____ My family

5. Who are you? _____ Sim

Writing Names of Pets

The names of pets also begin with a capital letter. The first letter in each name is a capital letter.

Examples:

   Winky   Silver   Rin Tin Tin

DIRECTIONS Name each pet. Use a name from the box. Write each name under the pet. Begin each name with a capital letter.

| chip | muff | king | jet | goldy | speedy |

1.
_____

2.
_____

3.
_____

4.
_____

5.
_____

6.
_____

Writing Names of the Days

The names of the days of the week begin with a capital letter.
The first letter in each name is a capital letter.

Examples:

Sunday   Monday

Tuesday   Wednesday

Thursday Friday

Saturday

August						
Sun	Mon	Tues	Wed	Thur	Fri	Sat
			1	2	3	4
5	6	7	8	9	10	11
12	13	14	15	16	17	18
19	20	21	22	23	24	25
26	27	28	29	30	31	

DIRECTIONS **Answer each question. Write the name of a day of the week. Begin each name with a capital letter.**

1. What day comes before Tuesday? _____

2. What day comes after Thursday? _____

3. What day comes before Monday? _____

4. What day begins with the letter <u>W</u>? _____

5. What two days start with the letter <u>T</u>?

_____   _____

6. What two days start with the letter <u>S</u>?

_____   _____

Writing Names of the Months

The names of the months of the year begin with a capital letter.
The first letter in each name is a capital letter.
Examples:

June   August   November

DIRECTIONS   **Read the name of each month. Then, rewrite each name. Begin each name with a capital letter.**

1. january

2. february

3. march

4. april

5. may

6. june

7. july

8. august

9. september

10. october

11. november

12. december

Practice with Names of the Months

Remember, the names of the months of the year begin with a capital letter. The first letter in each name is a capital letter.

DIRECTIONS ➤ Answer each question with the name of a month. Begin each name with a capital letter.

1. What month were you born?

2. What month did school begin?

3. What is the first month in a year?

4. What is the last month in a year?

5. What month do you like best?

Writing Names of Holidays

The names of holidays begin with a capital letter. The first letter in each important part of the name is a capital letter.

Examples:

New Year's Day
Fourth of July
Earth Day

EARTH DAY

DIRECTIONS Read each sentence. Write the name of each holiday correctly. Begin each important part of the name with a capital letter.

1. I get cards on valentine's day.

_____

_____

2. Let's plant a tree on arbor day.

_____

_____

3. Dad likes independence day.

_____

_____

4. Did you go away on thanksgiving day?

_____

_____

5. I like to dress up on halloween.

_____

_____

Writing Names of Special Places

The names of special places begin with a capital letter. Some special places are streets, cities, and states. The first letter in each part of the name is a capital letter.

Examples:

First Street   New York City   Florida

DIRECTIONS ▶ **Read each sentence. Underline the names of streets, cities, or states. Then, rewrite each sentence correctly. Use capital letters where they are needed.**

1 Billy lives on jane street.

_____

_____

2. My uncle lives on river road.

_____

_____

3. I live on lake drive.

_____

_____

4. Diane lives in boston.

_____

_____

5. Ed took a trip to los angeles.

_____

_____

6. My brother works in texas.

_____

_____

Practice with Special Place Names

Remember, the names of streets, cities, states, and countries begin with a capital letter. The first letter in each part of the name is a capital letter.

DIRECTIONS → **Answer each question with a special place name. Begin each name with a capital letter.**

1. What is the name of the street where you live?

_____

_____

2. What is the name of the city or town where you live?

_____

_____

3. What is the name of the state where you live?

_____

_____

4. What is the name of the country where you live?

_____

_____

Writing Titles of Books

Begin the first word, last word, and all important words in a book title with a capital letter. Underline the title of a book.
Examples:

<u>The Silver Pony</u>
<u>Peas at Supper</u>
<u>Billy and Blaze</u>

DIRECTIONS ➤ **Read each book title. Then, rewrite each title correctly. Use capital letters where they are needed. Underline each title that you write.**

1. red flags

_____

2. the black horse

_____

3. dad and me

_____

4. flowers for mom

_____

5. first grade day

_____

Period

Use a **period (.)** at the end of a telling sentence.
Example:
    I can swing.
Use a period at the end of the titles of people.
Examples:
    Mr.   Mrs.   Ms.   Dr.
    Mr. Hill went to see Dr. Green.

DIRECTIONS **Write each sentence correctly.**

1. The bears play a game

_____

2. They throw a ball

_____

3. Mrs Bear came home

_____

4. Mr Frog came to visit

_____

Question Mark

Use a **question mark (?)** at the end of an asking sentence.
Examples:
    Will it rain today?
    Where do the clouds go?

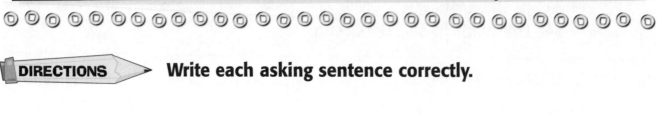

DIRECTIONS ▸ Write each asking sentence correctly.

1. Why is the sky blue

_____

_ _

_____

2. How do flowers grow

_____

_ _

_____

3. Where do the stars go

_____

_ _

_____

4. Why do the birds sing

_____

_ _

_____

5. When will the sun shine

_____

_ _

_____

Comma

Use a **comma (,)** between the day and the year in a date.

Examples:

July 4, 1776   November 18, 2004

ⓓ ⓓ

DIRECTIONS ➤ **Read each sentence. Circle the date. Then, write the date correctly. Remember to use a capital letter to begin the name of the month.**

1. I got a letter on may 23 2005.

_____

_____

2. Jan had a party on january 1 2005.

_____

_____

3. Kim was born on june 30 1997.

_____

_____

4. Leo got a new puppy on october 31 2003.

_____

_____

5. Today is _____.

Rhyming Words

Words that end with the same sounds are **rhyming words**.
Here are some rhyming words.
Examples:

car—star   boat—goat   top—drop

DIRECTIONS Read each sentence. Look at the word in dark print.
Choose the word in ( ) that ends with the same sound.
Write the rhyming word on the line.

1. It is lots of **fun**

To play in the _____.
(sand, sun)

2. I can run and **hide**

And go down the _____.
(slide, sled)

3. Our new gray **cat**

Lay on a soft _____.
(mat, mop)

4. The little black **bug**

Went under the _____.
(rag, rug)

5. A big green **frog**

Sat on a _____.
(log, lap)

Practice with Rhyming Words

Remember, words that end with
the same sound are **rhyming words.**
Examples:
     pin—win   bug—rug

DIRECTIONS > **Draw a line between rhyming words.**

1. pig   sock

2. door   flat

3. bat   big

4. clock   fan

5. man   floor

DIRECTIONS > **Write a funny sentence using one of the rhyming pairs you made.**

6. _____

_____

_____

_____

Rhymes

A **rhyme** is a short poem. The lines end with rhyming words. Many rhymes are silly or funny.
Example:
The cat took a rocket trip to the moon.
It left in July and came back in June.

DIRECTIONS **Complete the rhymes. You may use the words in the box.**

snow	me	night	sky

1. I wonder where the flowers go

_____

Every time it starts to _____.

2. Would you like to fly up high

_____

And ride a cloud across the _____?

3. I would like to ask a bee

_____

To make some honey just for _____.

4. Why does the sun's light

_____

Go away every _____?

Words That Mean the Same

Some words mean almost the same thing.
Example:
    hop—jump

 **DIRECTIONS** **Change the word in dark print to a word that means almost the same thing. Use the words in the box.**

catch	road	big	home

1. The man ran from his **house**. _____

2. He skipped down the **street**. _____

3. The dog could not **get** him. _____

4. The dog was **large**. _____

Words That Mean the Same, page 2

Remember, some words mean almost the same thing.
Example:
    look—watch

Read each pair of sentences. Look at the word in dark print in the first sentence. Circle a word in the second sentence that means almost the same thing. Write both words on the line.

1. I hear a **sound**. The noise is my puppy.

_____

2. I **begin** to call his name. My puppy starts to bark.

_____

3. I **look** under my bed. I see him there.

_____

4. He is **glad** to see me. I am happy, too.

_____

5. My puppy is **little**. He is a small dog.

_____

More Words That Mean the Same, page 3

Some words mean almost the same thing.
Example:
    talk–chat

DIRECTIONS Read the clues. Fill in the puzzle with words from the box.

small   sad   silly   yell   skinny

Down

1. This word means

   the same as **thin**.

3. This word means

   the same as **funny**.

4. This word means

   the same as **unhappy**.

Across

2. This word means the

   same as **shout**.

3. This word means the same as **tiny**.

Words That Mean the Opposite

Some words have opposite meanings.
Example:
    happy—sad

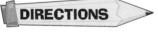 **DIRECTIONS** Read each sentence. Look at the word in dark print.
Circle the word in ( ) that means the opposite.

1. Pete went **up** the stairs. (down, out)

2. He sat on his **soft** bed. (new, hard)

3. Soon it was **dark** outside. (light, cold)

4. He turned **on** the lamp. (red, off)

5. Pete looked **out** the window. (in, off)

6. He **closed** his eyes. (rubbed, opened)

7. Soon Pete was **asleep**. (hungry, awake)

Words That Mean the Opposite, page 2

Remember, some words have opposite meanings.
Examples:

    up—down   hot—cold

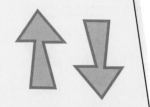

 **DIRECTIONS** Read each sentence. Look at the word in dark print. Choose a word from the box that means the opposite. Write the word on the line.

down	in	big	new	soft	off

1. I am **little**, and my sister is _____.

2. When I go **out**, she comes _____.

3. Her bike is **old**, but mine is _____.

4. First I get **on** my bike, then I get _____.

5. I go **up** the steps and _____ the slide.

6. I have a **hard** apple, and she has a _____ cookie.

More Words That Mean the Opposite, page 3

Some words have opposite meanings.
Example:
    cold—hot

DIRECTIONS   Read the clues. Fill in the puzzle with words from the box.

wet	wrong	slow	young	tiny

Across

1. This is the opposite of **dry**.

2. This is the opposite of **fast**.

4. This is the opposite of **old**.

Down

1. This is the opposite

    of **right**.

3. This is the opposite

    of **huge**.

Words That Sound Alike

Some words sound alike, but they have different meanings.
Think about what you read carefully.
Examples:

      hear—here   there—their

DIRECTIONS **Read each pair of sentences. Circle the words in each pair that sound alike.**

1. I know what Jane said.
She told her dog "no."

2. I yelled "hi" to Bill.
He waved to me from a high window.

3. I had eight bugs.
My frog ate seven of them.

4. Mom bakes cookies with flour.
She draws a flower with pink icing.

5. I love to go to the sea.
I like to see the boats.

6. My mother went to a sale.
She got a sail for my boat.

7. I read a story yesterday.
It was about a red dog.

8. I cannot hear you.
Come over here.

Words That Sound Alike, page 2

Some words sound alike, but they have different meanings.
To and <u>two</u> sound alike. They mean different things.
Examples:

      I went **to** my aunt's house.
      She gave me **two** gifts.

DIRECTIONS   Complete each sentence. Circle the correct word in ( ).

1. I took a ball (to, two) Ben.

2. Now he has (to, two) balls.

3. Ben went (to, two) the game.

4. He ate (to, two) hot dogs.

5. He wants (to, two) play ball.

6. I have (to, two) hands.

7. I used them (to, two) clap.

8. My house has (to, two) doors.

Practice with <u>Their</u> and <u>There</u>

Remember, some words sound alike, but they have different meanings. <u>Their</u> and <u>there</u> sound alike. They mean different things. <u>Their</u> shows that something belongs to two or more people.

Example:

They gave **their** dog a bath.

<u>There</u> shows a place. <u>There</u> is also used before <u>is</u> or <u>are</u>.

Example:

Put the books **there**.

There are two cats on the window.

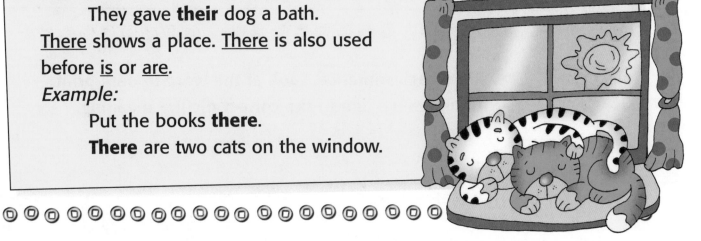

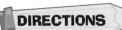 **DIRECTIONS**   **Complete each sentence. Circle the correct word in ( ).**

1. The family got into (there, their) car.

2. The children hung up (there, their) coats.

3. Do you live (there, their)?

4. Mia and Dan played in (there, their) tree house.

5. (There, Their) are many kids in the park today.

Choosing the Right Meaning

Some words are spelled alike, but they have different meanings.
Examples:

    roll—kind of bread   I had a **roll** for lunch.

    roll—turn over and over   I like to **roll** down the hill.

DIRECTIONS Read each sentence. Look at the word in dark print. Then, draw a line to the correct picture meaning.

1. Tony hit the ball with a **bat**.

2. The **bat** flies in the dark.

    a.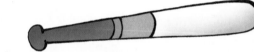

3. Juan plays ball with a heavy **bat**.

4. How does a **bat** see at night?

    b.

---

5. The **duck** made a loud quack.

6. We had to **duck** under the fence.

    a.

7. We were asked to **duck**

   so they could see.

    b.

8. The **duck** swam in the water.

Words That Show Order

Some words tell about **order**. Some order words are <u>first</u>, <u>next</u>, <u>then</u>, and <u>last</u>.

Example:

first	next	then	last

DIRECTIONS ▷ **Complete the story. Use the words <u>First</u>, <u>Next</u>, <u>Then</u>, and <u>Last</u>.**

Jack the Bear had a loose tooth.

_____
_____ he wiggled his tooth.

_____
_____ it fell out.

_____
_____ he put his tooth under his pillow.

_____
_____ he found a toy under his pillow.

Practice with Words That Show Order

Remember, some words tell about order. Some order words
are <u>first</u>, <u>next</u>, <u>then</u>, and <u>last</u>.

Look at each picture. Write a sentence for each order
word to make a story.

1. First _____

_____

2. Next _____

_____

3. Then _____

_____

4. Last _____

_____

Compound Words

A **compound word** is made of two words. The two words are put together to make a new word.
Examples:

> song + bird = songbird
> bed + room = bedroom
> every + thing = everything

DIRECTIONS ▸ **Complete each sentence. Use a compound word from the box.**

sandbox	backyard	birdhouse

1. There are two trees in my _____.

2. There is a _____ in one tree.

3. I like to play in my _____.

DIRECTIONS ▸ **Write a sentence. Use a compound word.**

4. _____

More Compound Words

Remember, a compound word is made of two words.
The two words are put together to make a new word.
Example:

    star + fish = starfish

DIRECTIONS ▶ **Draw a line between two words that make a new compound word.**

1. rain   shine

2. sea   bow

3. sail   boat

4. sun   shell

DIRECTIONS ▶ **Can you think of another compound word? Write it here.**

5. _____

Writing Sentences with Naming Words

A sentence is a group of words. It tells a complete idea.
A sentence begins with a capital letter.
A naming word tells about a person, place, or thing.
Example:

The black **dog** barks.

 **DIRECTIONS** Complete each sentence. Choose a naming word from the box. Write it on the line.

flowers	garden	rain	seeds	store	sun

1. Jo went to the _____.

2. She got some little brown _____.

3. Jo will plant the seeds in the _____.

4. The _____ will fall on the garden.

5. The _____ will warm the garden.

6. Pretty _____ will grow in the garden.

Writing Sentences with Action Words

A sentence tells a complete idea. A sentence begins with a capital letter.

An action word tells what something or someone does.

Example:

Barry **drinks** some juice.

DIRECTIONS > Complete each sentence. Choose an action word from the box. Write it on the line.

bark	climbs	chase	eat	jump	run

1. The two dogs _____ fast.

2. The dogs _____ up.

3. They _____ their food.

4. The dogs _____ the cat.

5. The dogs _____ loudly.

6. The cat _____ a tree.

Writing Sentences

A sentence tells a complete idea. A sentence begins with a capital letter. It has a naming part and a telling part.

Example:

Naming part	Telling part
The children	rode a bus to school.

DIRECTIONS Look at the sentence parts in the box. Draw a line from a naming part to a telling part. Then, write the sentence on the line. Be sure to put a period at the end of the sentence.

Naming part	Telling part
1. The birds	digs
2. That frog	swims
3. The fish	hops
4. My dog	fly

1. _____

2. _____

3. _____

4. _____

Writing More Sentences

A sentence tells a complete idea. It begins with a capital letter. A telling sentence ends with a period.
Example:
I am reading.

DIRECTIONS ➤ **Write a telling sentence to answer each question.**

1. Are you a girl or a boy?

_____

- -

_____

2. Are you sitting or standing?

_____

- -

_____

3. Do you use a pen or a pencil?

_____

- -

_____

4. Do you walk or ride to school?

_____

- -

_____

5. Is it day or night now?

_____

- -

_____

6. Is it cold or hot today?

_____

- -

_____

Practice with Writing Sentences

Remember, a sentence tells a complete idea.
It begins with a capital letter. A telling sentence ends
with a period.
Example:
>   I like to dive.

DIRECTIONS ▷   **Write a telling sentence to answer each question.**

1. How old are you?

_____

_____

2. Where do you live?

_____

_____

3. What do you like to play?

_____

_____

4. What do you like to eat?

_____

_____

5. What do you like to wear?

_____

_____

6. Where do you like to go?

_____

_____

Writing Sentences About a Picture

A sentence tells a complete idea. It begins with a capital letter.
It has a naming part and a telling part.

○○○○○○○○○○○○ ○○○○○○○○○○ ○○○○○○○○○ ○○○ ○

DIRECTIONS Look at the picture carefully. Then, write at least
three sentences that tell about the picture.

_____

_____

_____

_____

_____

_____

_____

Paragraphs

A **paragraph** is a group of sentences. The sentences tell about one main idea. The first line of a paragraph is indented. This means the first word is moved in a little from the left margin.

The first sentence in a paragraph tells the main idea. The other sentences tell about the main idea.

Example:

> **Red Creek School is finished.** The inside is nice and bright. The playground is very big. The school will open very soon. You will like the new school.

How to Write a Paragraph

1. Write a sentence that tells the main idea.
2. Indent the first line.
3. Write sentences that tell more about the main idea.

DIRECTIONS ▸ **Write sentences that tell about this main idea.**

I like school.

Writing a Story About You

A **story about you** is one kind of story you can write. In a story about you, you tell about something you did.
Example:

> I like to dive. I practice every day. At the pool I climb the ladder. Then, I walk to the end of the diving board. I put my arms up, and I dive. Splash! Into the water I go.

How to Write a Story About You
1. Think about things you have done.
2. Choose one thing to write about.
3. Begin your story.
4. Tell in order what you did.
5. Use words like <u>I</u> and <u>me</u>.

DIRECTIONS **Answer the question.**

What is the main idea of the example story? (Remember, the main idea is the first sentence of the paragraph.)

_____

_____

_____

Writing a Story About You, page 2

DIRECTIONS Think about something you have done. Write a story about you. Write your main idea in the first sentence. Indent the first sentence. Give your story a title. Draw a picture to go with your story.

_____

- -

_____

- -

_____

- -

_____

- -

_____

- -

_____

Writing a Poem

A **poem** makes a picture with words. Some poems have rhyming words. Rhyming words end with the same sound.

Example:

Home in the Sea

Dolphins and whales
So happy and free,
I wish I could go
To your home in the sea.

How to Write a Poem
1. Try to paint a picture with words.
2. End some lines with rhyming words.
3. Give your poem a title.

> **DIRECTIONS** Complete the poem. Use rhyming words. Give the poem a title.

_____

I wish I could be

_____

As tall as a _____.

I wish I could fly

_____

As high as the _____.

Writing a Poem, page 2

DIRECTIONS Think about something you like. Write a poem about it. Use some rhyming words. Give your poem a title. Draw a picture to go with your poem.

Writing a Description

In a **description**, you tell about something. You use words that tell how the thing looks, sounds, tastes, smells, or feels.
Example:

The Fish Store

Our class went to a fish store. It was small and dark inside. There were many pretty fish. We watched a girl feed the fish. Then they swam fast!

How to Write a Description
1. Think about things you have seen.
2. Choose one to write about.
3. Write a sentence that tells what you are describing.
4. Write sentences that tell what the thing was like.
5. Use describing words. Give details about how the thing looked, sounded, tasted, smelled, or felt.
6. Give your description a title.

DIRECTIONS Complete the sentence.

One describing word in the story is _____.

Writing a Description, page 2

DIRECTIONS → Think about something you have seen. Write a description of it. Use describing words. Write your main idea in the first sentence. Indent the first sentence. Give your description a title. Draw a picture to go with your description.

Writing a Friendly Letter

You can write a **friendly letter** to someone you know. In it, you tell about yourself. A friendly letter has five parts. They are the heading, greeting, body, closing, and signature.

Example:

heading → July 27, 2005

greeting → Dear Sam,

body →   I like my new house. At first, I was lonely. Then I met Jake. We played ball. Now he is my friend. And so are you!

closing → Your friend,

signature → Danny

How to Write a Friendly Letter
1. Choose a friend to write to.
2. Write about things you have done.
3. Use capital letters and commas correctly.
4. Use the five parts that are shown by the arrows.

DIRECTIONS > **Answer the question.**

_____

Who wrote this letter? _____

Writing a Friendly Letter, page 2

DIRECTIONS Think about something you have done. Think of a friend to write to in a letter. Write a letter to your friend. Use capital letters and commas correctly. Be sure to use the five parts of a friendly letter.

Writing a How-to Paragraph

A **how-to paragraph** tells how to do or make something. The steps are told in order.

Example:

I can play hide-and-seek. You can play it, too. You will need places to hide. You also need some friends to play with. First, close your eyes. Then, count to ten while your friends hide. Last, go and find your friends.

How to Write a How-To Paragraph
1. Think about things you know how to do.
2. Choose one thing to write about.
3. Write how to do that thing.
4. Tell the things you will need to do it.
5. Tell the steps in the right order.
6. Use words like <u>first</u> and <u>last</u>.

 **DIRECTIONS** **Answer the question.**

What does the example paragraph tell how to do?

_____

_____

_____

DIRECTIONS Think about something you know how to do. Write a paragraph telling how to do it. Write what you will tell about in the first sentence. Indent the first sentence. Tell what is needed to do the thing. Use order words. Draw a picture to go with your how-to paragraph.

Writing a Book Report

A **book report** tells about a book you have read.
Example:

<u>Birthday Cookies</u>
by Ann Wilson

<u>Birthday Cookies</u> is about Tom. He and his mother bake lots of cookies. Tom takes them to school for his birthday. My favorite part is when the other children eat all the cookies. I really liked this book.

How to Write a Book Report
1. Write the title of the book. Underline it.
2. Write the author's name.
3. Tell who or what the book is about.
4. Tell your favorite part.
5. Tell what you think about the book.

 **DIRECTIONS** Answer the question.

What is the title of the book in the book report?

_____

_ _

_____

Writing a Book Report, page 2

DIRECTIONS Think about a book you have read. Write a paragraph telling about the book. Tell the name of the book and who wrote it. Tell what happens in the book. Tell your favorite part. Tell if you liked the book. Indent the first sentence. Draw a picture to go with your book report.

ABC Order

The order of letters from <u>A</u> to <u>Z</u> is called **ABC order**.

a b c d e f g h i j k l m n
o p q r s t u v w x y z

ant

bear

cat

DIRECTIONS   Write the letters in ABC order.

1. a c b

2. f h g

3. c e d

4. p n o

5. i h j

6. z x y

ABC Order, page 2

Remember, the order of letters from <u>A</u> to <u>Z</u> is called ABC order. Words can be in ABC order, too. Use the first letter of a word to put it in ABC order.

Examples:

big	**c**at	**d**og
fish	**m**an	**s**un

DIRECTIONS Look at each group of words. Look at the letters in dark print. Put the words in ABC order. Write the words in ABC order on the lines.

1. a b c d e f

can **b**ird **d**ig

_____

_____

_____

2. e f g h i j

give **h**elp **f**ind

_____

_____

_____

3. m n o p q r

red **o**ne **n**ame

_____

_____

_____

4. s t u v w x

we **s**he **t**hey

_____

_____

_____

ABC Order, page 3

Remember, the order of letters from <u>A</u> to <u>Z</u> is called ABC order. Words can be in ABC order, too. Use the first letter of a word to put it in ABC order.

DIRECTIONS

First, number the words in ABC order. Then, write the words in order to make sentences. Be sure to put a period at the end of each sentence.

1. _____ likes   _____ me   _____ He

_____

_____

2. _____ Dave   _____ playing   _____ is

_____

_____

3. _____ outside   _____ Anna   _____ goes

_____

_____

4. _____ Mouse   _____ Cat   _____ finds

_____

_____

Parts of a Book

The **title page** is in the front of a book. It tells the title of the book. It tells who wrote the book. And it tells what company published the book.

 **DIRECTIONS** Look at this title page from a book about dogs. Then, answer the questions.

ALL ABOUT DOGS
by
Minnie Fleas

Barker Books
New York

1. What is the title of the book?

_____

_____

2. Who wrote the book?

_____

_____

3. What company published the book?

_____

_____

Parts of a Book, page 2

Some books have many stories or chapters. The **contents** of a book tells where each story or chapter begins.

DIRECTIONS Look at the picture of the book. Write the page number where each chapter begins.

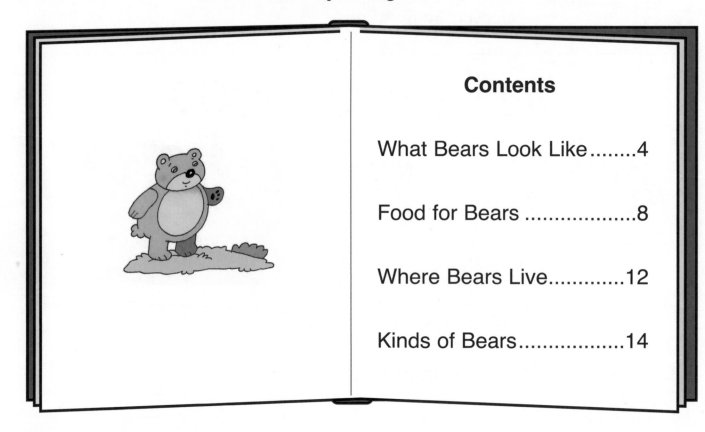

Contents

What Bears Look Like........4

Food for Bears 8

Where Bears Live............12

Kinds of Bears................14

1. Food for Bears _____	**2.** Where Bears Live _____
3. What Bears Look Like _____	**4.** Kinds of Bears _____

Order of Events

The sentences in a story tell things in the order they happen.
Words such as <u>first</u>, <u>next</u>, <u>then</u>, and <u>last</u> help tell when things happen.
Example:

Brett got ready for bed. **First**, she took a bath. **Next**, she brushed her teeth. **Then**, she put on her pajamas. **Last**, she read a story and got into bed.

 **DIRECTIONS** ▷ **Read the story. Then, number the sentences. Write *1, 2, 3,* or *4* to show what happened first, second, third, and last.**

Carla planted flowers. First, she got a shovel. Next, she dug some holes in the garden. Then, she put the flowers into the holes. Last, she put the shovel back in its place.

_____ First, she got a shovel.

_____ Then, she put the flowers into the holes.

_____ Last, she put the shovel back in its place.

_____ Next, she dug some holes in the garden.

Conclusions

A **conclusion** is a decision you make. You look at the facts. You think carefully. Then, you decide. You make a conclusion.
Example:

   It has many teeth, but it cannot bite. What is it?
   Answer: a comb.

DIRECTIONS Read each animal riddle. Write the name of the animal.

| bird | rabbit | monkey | whale |

1. This animal is very big.
   It lives in the water, but
   it is not a fish.
   What is it?

   _____

2. This animal can hop fast.
   It has a small, fluffy tail.
   It eats in my garden!
   What is it?

   _____

3. This animal can climb.
   It has a long tail.
   It lives in the tops of trees.
   What is it?

   _____

4. This animal sits on a branch.
   It makes a nest.
   It can fly up high.
   What is it?

   _____

Practice with Conclusions

Remember, to make a conclusion you look at the facts. You think carefully. Then, you decide.

DIRECTIONS ➤ **Read each riddle. Write the name of the thing.**

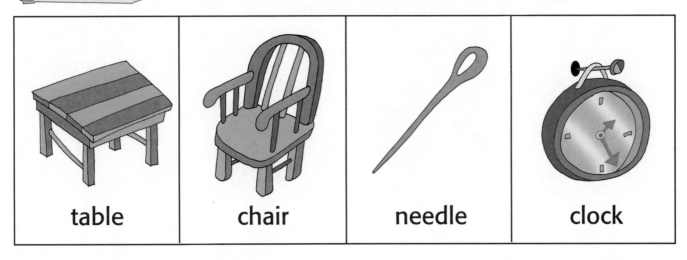

| table | chair | needle | clock |

1. You can eat on this thing. It has legs but cannot walk. What is it?

_____

_ _ _ _ _ _ _ _ _ _ _

2. You can sew with this thing. It has an eye but cannot see. What is it?

_ _ _ _ _ _ _ _ _ _ _ _ _

3. This thing tells time. It has hands but cannot clap. What is it?

_ _ _ _ _ _ _ _ _ _ _ _

4. You can sit in this thing. It has arms but cannot carry anything. What is it?

_ _ _ _ _ _ _ _ _ _ _ _ _

Classifying

Classify means to put things in groups. Think how things are alike. Then, you can put them in groups together.

ⓞ ⓞ

DIRECTIONS ▸ **Look at the drawings. Think. How are the animals in each group alike? Write the word.**

1. Animals that _____

2. Animals that _____

DIRECTIONS ▸ **Draw a picture of another animal for each group.**

Comparing and Contrasting

Compare means to tell how things are alike. **Contrast** means to tell how things are different.

 **DIRECTIONS** Look at the two pictures. Think. How are they different? How are they alike? Write one sentence telling how they are alike. Write one sentence telling how they are different.

More Comparing and Contrasting

Remember that compare means to tell how things are alike. Contrast means to tell how things are different.

DIRECTIONS > Draw a picture of you and your best friend. Write one sentence about how you are alike. Write one sentence about how you are different.

Summarizing

Summarizing means to tell what happens in a story in your own words.

○○

> **DIRECTIONS** **Read the story. Then, complete the story map.**

Matt's Birthday

Matt the Mouse was sad. Today was his birthday. He could not find any of his friends. He went for a walk in the garden. He looked at the plants. They were moving!

"Who is back there?" called Matt.

"Surprise!" shouted all his friends. "Happy birthday, Matt!"

"Thank you!" Matt smiled.

1. Who? _____

2. Where? _____

3. What happened first? _____

_____

4. What happened next? _____

_____

5. What happened at the end? _____

_____

Fact or Fantasy?

Some stories tell **facts** about things. Facts are things that could really happen.

Some stories tell about things that could not happen. These stories are called **fantasy**.

DIRECTIONS   Read each sentence. Could it really happen? Circle <u>yes</u> if the sentence is a fact. Circle <u>no</u> if the sentence is not a fact.

1. Sandy picks a flower.	yes	no
2. The flower starts to cry.	yes	no
3. A bee lands on a leaf.	yes	no
4. The leaf says, "You're heavy!"	yes	no
5. Sandy follows the bee.	yes	no
6. The bee smiles at Sandy.	yes	no
7. The bee reads a story.	yes	no
8. Sandy falls asleep.	yes	no

Fact or Fantasy?, page 2

Remember, some stories tell facts about things. Facts are things that could really happen.
Some stories tell about things that could not happen. These stories are called fantasy.

DIRECTIONS Read each sentence. Could it really happen? Circle <u>yes</u> if the sentence is a fact. Circle <u>no</u> if the sentence is not a fact.

1. We go to the circus on Saturday.   yes   no
2. The horses greet us and shake our hands.   yes   no

3. My cat flies around the room.   yes   no
4. He purrs when I pet him.   yes   no

5. I like to eat peanut butter and jelly.   yes   no
6. Peanut butter and jelly likes to eat cheese.   yes   no

7. A butterfly flies into the classroom!   yes   no
8. It raises its hand to answer a question.   yes   no

Answer Key

Unit 1

Page 6
1. boy, 2. girl, 3. dog, 4. cat

Page 7
1. man, 2. baby, 3. school, 4. store, 5. car, 6. fish

Page 8
1. doctor, 2. farmer, 3. worker, 4. cook

Page 9
Answers may vary. 1. fish, 2. frog, 3. fox, 4. bird, 5. dog, 6. cat

Page 10
1. lake, 2. house, 3. park, 4. farm

Page 11
1. cup, 2. crayons, 3. apple, 4. bed, 5. hat, 6. box

Page 12

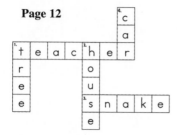

Page 13
1. Chris, 2. Lina, 3. Lee Chin, 4. Main Street, 5. "All About Worms"

Page 14
1. Sam, 2. Mr. Sosa, 3. Parker School, 4. Bakers Road

Page 15
1.–5. Answers will vary, but all names should begin with a capital letter.

Page 16
1. birds, 2. bug, 3. girls, 4. dog, 5. frogs

Page 17
1. trees, 2. flowers, 3. seeds, 4. nests

Page 18
1. I, 2. me, 3. I, 4. I, 5. me

Page 19
1. I, 2. me, 3. I, 4. me, 5. I

Page 20
1. We are here., 2. They are not here., 3. We will play ball., 4. They found a kitten.

Page 21
1. They are brothers., 2. We are sisters., 3. They are in second grade., 4. We are in first grade.

Page 22
1. She likes to write., 2. He likes to read., 3. It is on the table., 4. She saw the bird.

Page 23
1. He, 2. It, 3. She, 4. It, 5. She, 6. He

Page 24
1. eats, 2. waves, 3. talks, 4. sing, 5. ride

Page 25
1. The fish swims in the lake., 2. The rabbit hops up and down., 3. The snake crawls on the ground., 4. The birds fly in the sky.

Page 26
Action words and sentences will vary.

Page 27
Answers may vary. Possible responses are given. 1. jump, jumps, 2. roll, rolls, 3. bark, barks

Page 28
1. shines, 2. grow, 3. hops, 4. need, 5. gets

Page 29
Today is the first day of school. Madison eats pancakes. She puts on her dress and shoes. She and her sister walk to school. Madison finds her classroom. The teacher welcomes the students. The children smile at their new teacher. Madison thinks it will be a good year.

Page 30
1. Two little ducks played in the water., 2. The mother duck looked at them., 3. Two little ducks jumped out of the water., 4. They all walked away.

Page 31
1. fished, 2. watched, 3. listen, 4. painted, 5. cook

Page 32
1. is, 2. is, 3. are, 4. are, 5. are, 6. is

Page 33
Luke is very smart. We are best friends. We are in first grade. Mr. Jackson is our teacher. We are learning about birds. Luke is making a birdhouse.

Page 34
1. was, 2. were, 3. were, 4. was, 5. was, 6. was

Page 35
Tyler and Haley were moving to a new house. Mom and Dad were filling the truck. Haley is putting her toys in a box. Tyler was cleaning his room. The children were ready to see their new home. They were also sad to leave their old house.

Page 36
1. ran, 2. run, 3. saw, 4. came, 5. come, 6–7. Sentences will vary.

Page 37
1. came, 2. see, 3. run, 4. ran, 5. saw, 6. come

Page 38
1. went, 2. went, 3. go, 4. went, 5. go, 6. go

Page 39
1. went, 2. go, 3. went, 4. go, 5. go, 6. went

Page 40
1. don't, 2. won't, 3. can't, 4. isn't, 5. haven't, 6. shouldn't

Page 41
1. shouldn't, 2. haven't, 3. isn't, 4. can't, 5. won't, 6. don't

Page 42
1. in, 2. on, 3. under, 4. up, 5. out

Page 43
1. on, 2. up, 3. under, 4. in

Page 44
1. green, 2. loud, 3. wet, 4. two, 5. blue, 6. funny

Page 45
1. sleepy, 2. sick, 3. hungry, 4. glad, 5. angry

Page 46
1. big, 2. small, 3. tall, 4. round, 5. Sentences will vary.

Page 47
Answers may vary. 1. green, 2. pink, 3. yellow, 4. blue, 5. white, 6. red

Page 48
1. one, 2. four, 3. two, 4. five, 5. seven

Page 49
1. sour, 2. fresh, 3. salty, 4. smoky, 5. Sentences will vary.

Page 50
1. soft, 2. quiet, 3. hot, 4. cold, 5. noisy

Page 51
1. cloudy, 2. snowy, 3. sunny, 4. rainy, 5. windy

Page 52
1.–6. Describing words will vary.

Page 53
1.–5. Answers will vary.

Page 54
1. smaller, 2. bigger, 3. biggest, 4. taller

Page 55
1.–4. Check to see that the correct picture is circled.

Page 56
1. a, 2. a, 3. an, 4. an, 5. a, 6. a, 7. an, 8. an

Page 57
a column: radio, bear, fish, lamp, queen
an column: uncle, airplane, ape, inch, ocean

Unit 2

Page 58
1. I see a lion., 2. Jan throws

the ball., **3.** I hear a bird., **4.** My cat can jump., **5.** The dog barks.

Page 59
1. yes, **2.** no, **3.** no, **4.** yes, **5.** yes, **6.** no, **7.** no, **8.** yes

Page 60
1. A frog, **2.** A cat, **3.** A dog, **4.** chew bones, **5.** eat worms, **6.** walks to school

Page 61
1. The fisherman gets a fish., **2.** The dancer spins on stage., **3.** The artist draws a picture., **4.** The doctor helps the sick girl.

Page 62
1. Rick, **2.** His mother, **3.** The bear, **4.** The monkey, **5.** The tiger, **6.** The turtle

Page 63
Answers may vary. **1.** My sister, **2.** Amy, **3.** The wind, **4.** The blue kite, **5.** The red kite

Page 64
1. found a puppy, **2.** ate some food, **3.** played with Anna, **4.** named the puppy Skip, **5.** threw the ball, **6.** ran after the ball

Page 65
Answers may vary. **1.** are fun to grow, **2.** will show you, **3.** plant seeds, **4.** waters the seeds, **5.** gives them light

Page 66
1.–8. Answers will vary. Be sure that a naming part is given.

Page 67
1.–8. Answers will vary. Be sure that a telling part is given.

Page 68
1. Jim swims fast., **2.** Jane can not swim., **3.** Mike likes art., **4.** Eva walks to town., **5.** Kim sees a bird., **6.** The birds sing to me.

Page 69
1. I have a pig., **2.** He and I play., **3.** He has a cold nose., **4.** My pig is my friend., **5.** We have fun.

Page 70
1.–3. Sentences will vary.

Page 71
1. What is your name?, **2.** Where do you live?, **3.** When is your birthday?, **4.** Do you have a pet?, **5.** Who is your best friend?

Page 72
Answers may vary. **1.** When, **2.** Who, **3.** What, **4.** Where, **5.** Who, **6.** What

Page 73
1. tell, **2.** ask, **3.** tell, **4.** ask, **5.** ask, **6.** tell, **7.** ask

Page 74
Answers will vary. Possible responses are given. **1.** cold, **2.** crunchy, **3.** three, **4.** brown, **5.** black, **6.** white, soft

Page 75
1. Turtle and Fox hid., **2.** Jon and Teri played ball., **3.** Brett and Max ate lunch., **4.** Cat and Frog played with Duck.

Page 76
Answers may vary slightly. **1.** Chet reads and writes., **2.** The ducks swim and quack., **3.** I found a coin and a comb., **4.** We will eat some cake and ice cream.

Unit 3

Page 77
1. The sun is hot., **2.** We will go home., **3.** You can come with us., **4.** I will get some water., **5.** Do you have a cup?, **6.** Where is the door?

Page 78
1.–4. Answers will vary. Be sure each sentence begins with "I can."

Page 79
1. Pat Long, **2.** Eva Ramos, **3.** Uncle Thomas, **4.** Will Smith, **5.** Ling Chung, **6.** Mori Adams

Page 80
1.–5. Answers will vary, but all names should begin with a capital letter.

Page 81
1.–6. Names given to animals will vary. Be sure each written answer begins with a capital letter.

Page 82
1. Monday, **2.** Friday, **3.** Sunday, **4.** Wednesday, **5.** Tuesday, Thursday, **6.** Sunday, Saturday

Page 83
1. January, **2.** February, **3.** March, **4.** April, **5.** May, **6.** June, **7.** July, **8.** August, **9.** September, **10.** October, **11.** November, **12.** December

Page 84
1.–5. Answers will vary, but all month names should begin with a capital letter.

Page 85
1. Valentine's Day, **2.** Arbor Day, **3.** Independence Day, **4.** Thanksgiving Day, **5.** Halloween

Page 86
1. jane street; Billy lives on Jane Street., **2.** river road; My uncle lives on River Road., **3.** lake drive; I live on Lake Drive., **4.** boston; Diane lives in Boston., **5.** los angeles; Ed took a trip to Los Angeles., **6.** texas; My brother works in Texas.

Page 87
1.–4. Answers will vary, but all place names should begin with a capital letter.

Page 88
1. <u>Red Flags</u>, **2.** <u>The Black Horse</u>, **3.** <u>Dad and Me</u>, **4.** <u>Flowers for Mom</u>, **5.** <u>First Grade Day</u>

Page 89
1. The bears play a game., **2.** They throw a ball., **3.** Mrs. Bear came home., **4.** Mr. Frog came to visit.

Page 90
1. Why is the sky blue?, **2.** How do flowers grow?, **3.** Where do the stars go?, **4.** Why do the birds sing?, **5.** When will the sun shine?

Page 91
1. may 23 2005; May 23, 2005, **2.** january 1 2005; January 1, 2005, **3.** june 30 1997; June 30, 1997, **4.** october 31 2003; October 31, 2003, **5.** Answers will vary.

Unit 4

Page 92
1. sun, **2.** slide, **3.** mat, **4.** rug, **5.** log

Page 93
1. pig/big, **2.** door/floor, **3.** bat/flat, **4.** clock/sock, **5.** man/fan, **6.** Sentences will vary.

Page 94
Answers may vary. **1.** snow, **2.** sky, **3.** me, **4.** night

Page 95
1. home, **2.** road, **3.** catch, **4.** big

Page 96
1. sound, noise; **2.** begin, starts; **3.** look, see; **4.** glad, happy; **5.** little, small

Page 97

Page 98
1. down, **2.** hard, **3.** light, **4.** off, **5.** in, **6.** opened, **7.** awake

Page 99
1. big, **2.** in, **3.** new, **4.** off, **5.** down, **6.** soft

Page 100

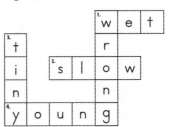

Page 101
1. know, no; **2.** hi, high; **3.** eight, ate; **4.** flour, flower; **5.** sea, see; **6.** sale, sail; **7.** read, red; **8.** hear, here

Page 102
1. to, 2. two, 3. to, 4. two, 5. to, 6. two, 7. to, 8. two

Page 103
1. their, 2. their, 3. there, 4. their, 5. There

Page 104
1. a, 2. b, 3. a, 4. b, 5. a, 6. b, 7. b, 8. a

Page 105
First, Next, Then, Last

Page 106
1.–4. Answers will vary.

Page 107
Answers may vary.
1. backyard, 2. birdhouse, 3. sandbox. 4. Sentences will vary.

Page 108
1. rainbow, 2. seashell, 3. sailboat, 4. sunshine, 5. Words will vary.

Unit 5
Page 109
Answers may vary. 1. store, 2. seeds, 3. garden, 4. rain, 5. sun, 6. flowers

Page 110
Answers may vary. 1. run, 2. jump, 3. eat, 4. chase, 5. bark, 6. climbs

Page 111
Answers may vary. 1. The birds fly., 2. That frog hops., 3. The fish swims., 4. My dog digs.

Page 112
1.–6. Answers will vary. Be sure each written response answers the question.

Page 113
1.–6. Answers will vary but all sentences should tell a complete thought, begin with a capital letter, and end with a period.

Page 114
Answers will vary.

Page 115
Answers will vary.

Page 116
Main Idea: The writer likes to dive.

Page 117
Answers will vary.

Page 118
Answers may vary. Possible answers: 1. tree, 2. sky

Page 119
Answers will vary.

Page 120
Answers will vary. Possible responses: small, dark, pretty, fast

Page 121
Answers will vary.

Page 122
Danny

Page 123
Answers will vary.

Page 124
play hide-and-seek

Page 125
Answers will vary.

Page 126
Birthday Cookies

Page 127
Answers will vary.

Unit 6
Page 128
1. a b c, 2. f g h, 3. c d e, 4. n o p, 5. h i j, 6. x y z

Page 129
1. bird, can, dig; 2. find, give, help; 3. name, one, red; 4. she, they, we

Page 130
1. 2, 3, 1; He likes me., 2. 1, 3, 2; Dave is playing., 3. 3, 1, 2; Anna goes outside., 4. 3, 1, 2; Cat finds Mouse.

Page 131
1. All About Dogs, 2. Minnie Fleas, 3. Barker Books

Page 132
1. 8, 2. 12, 3. 4, 4. 14

Page 133
1, 3, 4, 2

Page 134
1. whale, 2. rabbit, 3. monkey, 4. bird

Page 135
1. table, 2. needle, 3. clock, 4. chair

Page 136
1. swim, 2. fly

Page 137
Answers will vary. Possible responses: Alike: They are both tall., Different: They are made of different things.

Page 138
Answers will vary.

Page 139
1. Matt the Mouse; 2. in the garden; 3. Matt was sad because he couldn't find his friends on his birthday.; 4. He saw the plants move.; 5. His friends had a surprise birthday party for him.

Page 140
1. yes, 2. no, 3. yes, 4. no, 5. yes, 6. no, 7. no, 8. yes

Page 141
1. yes, 2. no, 3. no, 4. yes, 5. yes, 6. no, 7. yes, 8. no